It's Time to CROCHENIT™

General Information

Many of the products used in this pattern book can be purchased from local craft, fabric and variety stores, or from the Annie's Attic Needlecraft Catalog (see Customer Service information on page 32).

Contents

General Instructions

Pull up lp: Insert hook in designated lp, bar or st, yo, pull through *(see Photo A)*, leaving lp on hook.

A

Picking up lps: leave all lps on hook *(see Photo B)* unless otherwise stated.

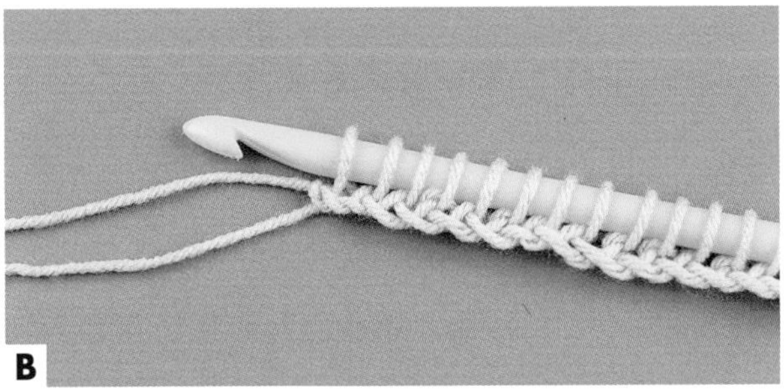
B

Turn: Rotate hook 180 degrees and slide all lps on hook to opposite end *(see Photo C)*. **Do not turn** unless otherwise stated.

C

Work lps off hook when adding a new color: With new color, place slip knot on hook, pull slip knot through one lp on hook *(see Photo D)*, [yo, pull through 2 lps on hook] across. Last lp rem on hook at end of row is first vertical bar of next row *(see Photo E)*.

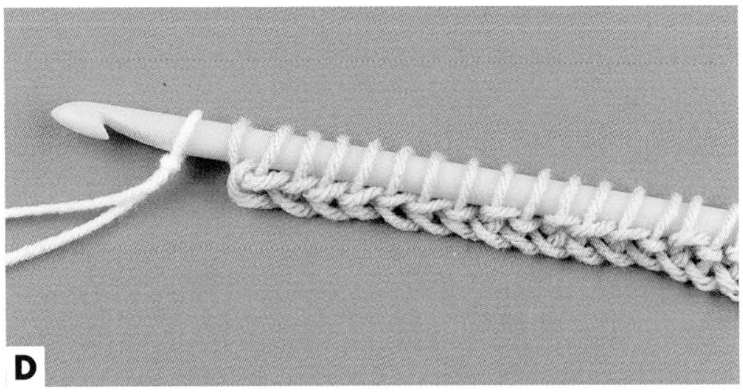
D

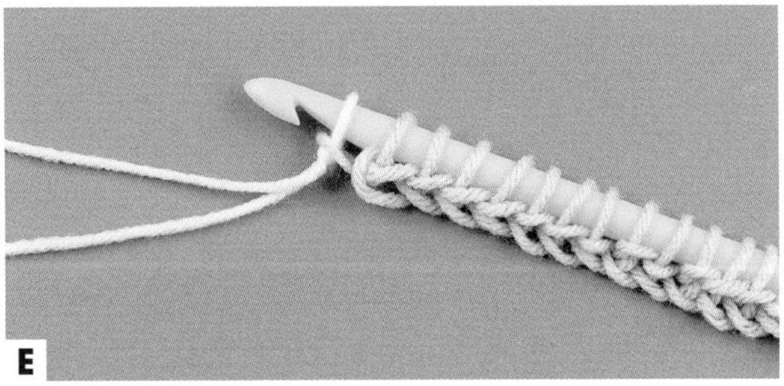
E

Work lps off hook with color already in use: Pick up color from row below, yo, pull through 1 lp on hook *(see Photo F)*, [yo, pull through 2 lps on hook] across.

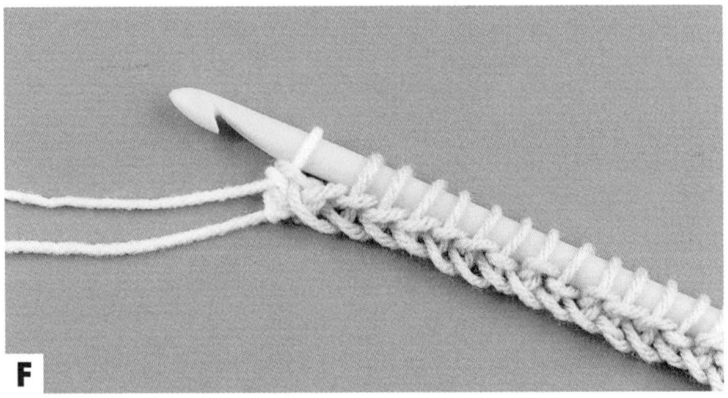
F

Fasten off color that is no longer needed: Work across the row as stated and cut yarn, leaving a long end, secure the end temporarily by tying to an adjacent yarn end, or ermanently by weaving back through an inch or so on the row before.

Working through the horizontal bar: Insert hook under only the top lp of the horizontal bar unless otherwise stated. ■

Green & White Place Mat & Trivet

DESIGN BY **CAROLYN CHRISTMAS**

SKILL LEVEL

INTERMEDIATE

FINISHED SIZES

Trivet: 10 x 11½ inches
Place Mat: 12 x 18 inches

MATERIALS

- Medium (worsted) weight cotton yarn:
  3½ oz/175 yds/100g pale green
- Medium (worsted) weight cotton yarn:
  3½ oz/175 yds/100g white
- Crochenit hook
- Size H/8/5mm crochet hook

4 MEDIUM

GAUGE

With Crochenit hook: 3 shells = 2 inches; 8 rows = 2 inches

PATTERN NOTES

Read General Instructions on page 2 before beginning pattern.

Fasten off colors when no longer needed.

Use Crochenit hook throughout unless otherwise stated.

Chain-3 at beginning of row or round counts as first double crochet unless otherwise stated.

Join with slip stitch as indicated unless otherwise stated.

SPECIAL STITCHES
Shell: (2 dc, ch 2, 2 dc) in place indicated.

Picot: Ch 3, sl st in 3rd ch form hook.

INSTRUCTIONS
TRIVET

Row 1: With white, ch 20, pull up lp in 2nd ch from hook, pull up lp in each ch across, turn. *(20 lps on hook)*

Row 2: With pale green, yo, pull through 1 lp on hook, yo, pull through 3 lps on hook *(this completes a ch-1 and a shell—see Photo A)*, *ch 1, yo, pull through 3 lps on hook *(this completes a ch-2 and a shell—see Photo B)*, rep from * 7 more times, yo, pull through last 2 lps on hook *(this completes ch-1 and a vertical bar)*, **do not turn.**

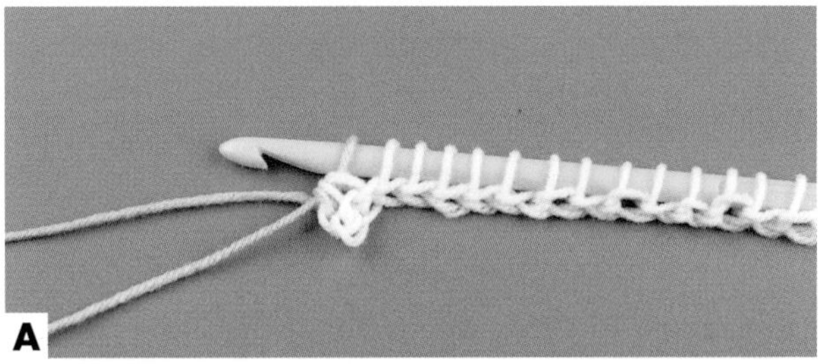
A

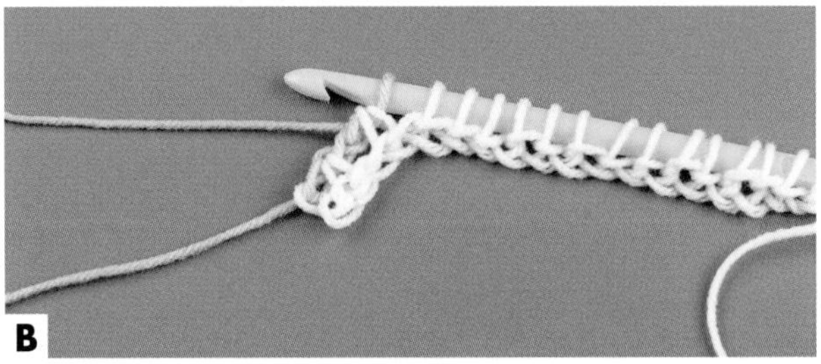
B

Row 3: Ch 1, sk shells, pull up lp in each ch across to last vertical bar *(see Photo C)*, pull up lp in last vertical bar, turn. *(20 lps on hook)*

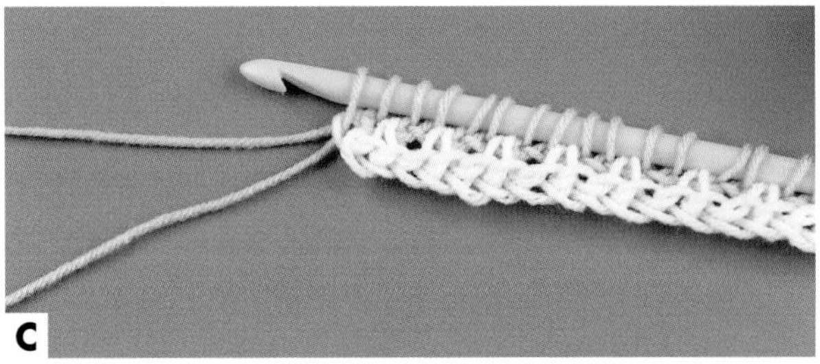
C

Row 4: With white, yo, pull through 1 lp on hook, yo, pull through 3 lps on hook, [ch 1, yo, pull through 3 lps on hook] 8 times, ch 1, yo, pull through last 2 lps on hook, **do not turn.**

Row 5: Ch 1, sk shells, pull up lp in each ch across, turn. *(20 lps on hook)*

Rows 6–36: [Rep rows 2–5 consecutively] 8 times, ending last rep with row 4.

Row 37: To bind off, ch 1, sl st in each ch across, sl st in last vertical bar. Fasten off.

EDGING

Rnd 1: Working around outer edge, with size H hook, **join** *(see Pattern Notes)* white yarn in first st of last row, **ch 3** *(see Pattern Notes)*, (dc, ch 1, 2 dc, ch 1, 2 dc) in same st *(corner)*, ch 1, sk next st, dc in next st, ch 1, sk next 3 sts, **shell** *(see Special Stitches)* in next st, ch 1, sk next 3 sts, dc in next st, ch 1, sk next 3 sts, shell in next st, ch 1, sk next 2 sts, dc in next st, ch 1, sk next st, (2 dc, ch 1, 2 dc, ch 1, 2 dc) in last st *(corner)*, working in ends of rows, ch 1, [dc in next white row, ch 1, shell in next white row, ch 1] 3 times, dc in next white row, ch 1, working in starting ch on opposite side of row 1, (2 dc, ch 1, 2 dc, ch 1, 2 dc) in first ch *(corner)*, ch 1, sk next ch, dc in next ch, ch 1, sk next 2 chs, shell in next ch, ch 1, sk next 3 chs, dc in next ch, ch 1, sk next 3 chs, shell in next ch, ch 1, sk next 3 chs, dc in next ch, ch 1, sk next ch, (2 dc, ch 1, 2 dc, ch 1, 2 dc) in last ch *(corner)*, working in ends of rows, ch 1, dc in next white row, [ch 1, shell in next white row, ch 1, dc in next white row] 3 times, ch 1, join in 3rd ch of beg ch-3. *(10 shells, 38 dc, 36 ch-1 sps)*

Rnd 2: Sl st in next st, ch 1, (sc, **picot**—*see Special Stitches*, sc) in next ch sp, ch 2, (sc, picot, sc) in next ch sp, [*ch 3, sk next 2 sts, sc in next st, ch 3, (sc, picot, sc) in ch sp of next shell*, rep between *, ch 3, sk next 2 sts, sc in next st, ch 3, sk next 2 sts, (sc, picot, sc) in next ch sp, ch 2, (sc, picot, sc) in next ch sp, rep between * 3 times, ch 3, sk next 2 sts, sc in next st, ch 3], sk next 2 sts, (sc, picot, sc) in next ch sp, ch 2, (sc, picot, sc) in next ch sp, rep between [ ], join beg sc. Fasten off.

PLACE MAT

Row 1: With white, ch 26, pull up lp in 2nd ch from hook, pull up lp in each ch across, turn. *(26 lps on hook)*

Row 2: With pale green, yo, pull through 1 lp on hook, yo, pull through 3 lps on hook *(this completes a ch-1 and a shell—see Photo A)*, *ch 1, yo, pull through 3 lps on hook *(this completes a ch-2 and a shell—see Photo B)*, rep from * 10 times, yo, pull through last 2 lps on hook *(this completes ch-1 and a vertical bar)*, do not turn.

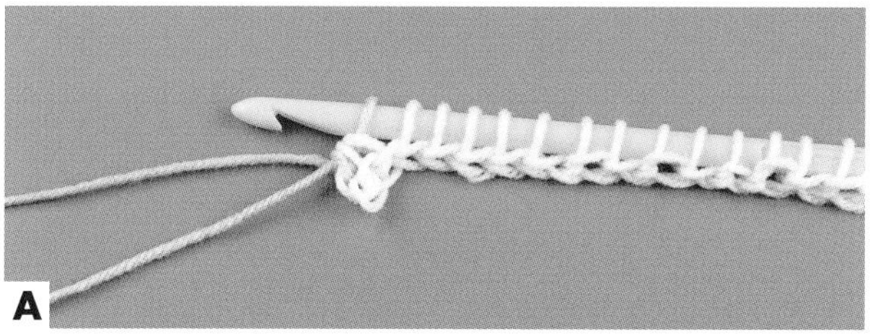
A

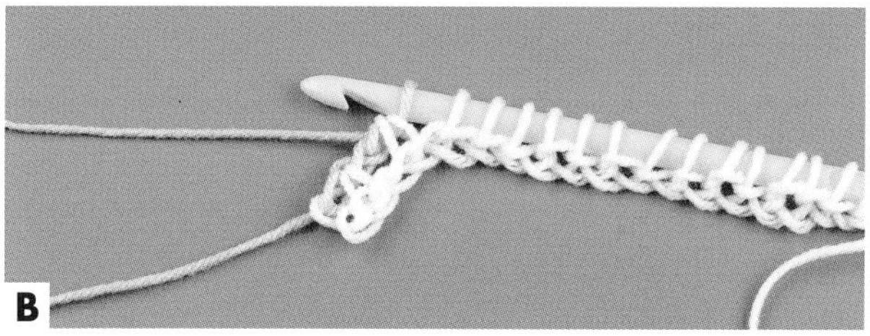
B

Row 3: Ch 1, sk shells, pull up lp in each ch across to last vertical bar *(see Photo C)*, pull up lp in last vertical bar, turn. *(26 lps on hook)*

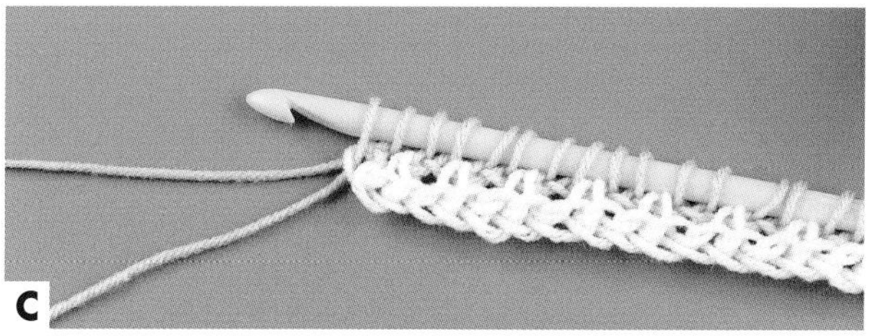
C

Row 4: With white, yo, pull through 1 lp on hook, yo, pull through 3 lps on hook, [ch 1, yo, pull through 3 lps on hook] 11 times, ch 1, yo, pull through last 2 lps on hook, do not turn.

Row 5: Ch 1, sk shells, pull up lp in each ch across, turn. *(26 lps on hook)*

Rows 6–60: [Rep rows 2–5 consecutively] 14 times, ending last rep with row 4.

Row 61: To bind off, ch 1, sl st in each ch across, sl st in last vertical bar. Fasten off.

EDGING

Rnd 1: Working around outer edge, with size H hook, **join** *(see Pattern Notes)* white in first st of last row, **ch 3** *(see Pattern Notes)*, (dc, ch 1, 2 dc, ch 1, 2 dc) in same st *(corner shell)*, *ch 1, sk next 2 sts, dc in next st, ch 1, sk next 2 sts, **shell** *(see Special Stitches)* in next ch sp, rep from *, ch 1, sk next 2 sts, dc in next st, ch 1, sk next 3 sts, shell in next st, ch 1, sk next 2 sts, dc in next st, ch 1, sk next 2 sts, (2 dc, ch 1, 2 dc, ch 1, 2 dc) in last st *(corner)*, working in ends of rows, ch 1, [dc in next white row, ch 1, shell in next white row, ch 1] 6 times, dc in next white row, ch 1, working in starting ch on opposite side of row 1, (2 dc, ch 1, 2 dc, ch 1, 2 dc) in first ch *(corner)*, ch 1, sk next 2 chs, dc in next ch, ch 1, sk next 2 chs, shell in next ch, ch 1, sk next 3 chs, dc in next ch, [ch 1, sk next 2 chs, shell in next ch, ch 1, sk next 2 chs, dc in next ch] 2 times, ch 1, sk next 2 chs, (2 dc, ch 1, 2 dc, ch 1, 2 dc) in last ch *(corner)*, working in ends of rows, ch 1, dc in next white row, [ch 1, shell in next white row, ch 1, dc in next white row] 6 times, ch 1, join in 3rd ch of beg ch-3. *(18 shells, 46 dc, 52 ch-1 sps)*

Rnd 2: Sl st in next st, ch 1, (sc, **picot**—*see Special Stitches*, sc) in next ch sp, ch 2, (sc, picot, sc) in next ch sp, [*ch 3, sk next 2 sts, sc in next st, ch 3, (sc, picot, sc) in ch sp of next shell*, rep between * twice, ch 3, sk next 2 sts, sc in next st, ch 3, sk next 2 sts, (sc, picot, sc) in next ch sp, ch 2, (sc, picot, sc) in next ch sp, rep between * 6 times, ch 3, sk next 2 sts, sc in next st, ch 3], sk next 2 sts, (sc, picot, sc) in next ch sp, ch 2, (sc, picot, sc) in next ch sp, rep between [ ], join in beg sc. Fasten off. ■

Candy Corn

DESIGN BY **SHIRLEY BROWN**

SKILL LEVEL

INTERMEDIATE

FINISHED SIZE

26 x 50 inches

MATERIALS

- Lily Sugar'n Cream Cotton medium (worsted) weight cotton yarn (2½ oz/120 yds/70g per ball):
  10 balls each #01130 warm brown and #00010 yellow
- Crochenit cable hook

4 MEDIUM

GAUGE

1 corn st = 1 inch; 2 rows = 1¼ inches

PATTERN NOTES

Read General Instructions on page 2 before beginning pattern.

Use rug backing on back of rugs that are placed on floors other than carpet.

SPECIAL STITCH

Corn stitch (corn st): Pull up lp in first ch of next ch-3, insert hook under top strand of 2 horizontal bars above next shell 3 rows below, yo, pull through, ch 1, pull up lp in last ch of same ch-3.

INSTRUCTIONS

RUG

Row 1: With warm brown, ch 103, working in **back bar of ch** *(see Fig. 1)*, pull up lp in 2nd ch from hook, pull up lp in each ch across, turn. *(103 lps on hook)*

Fig. 1
Back Bar of Chain

Row 2: With yellow, yo, pull through 1 lp on hook, yo, pull through 4 lps on hook *(this completes a ch-1 and a shell—see Photo A)*, *ch 2, yo, pull through 4 lps on hook *(this completes a ch-3 and a shell—see Photo B)*, rep from * across, **do not turn.**

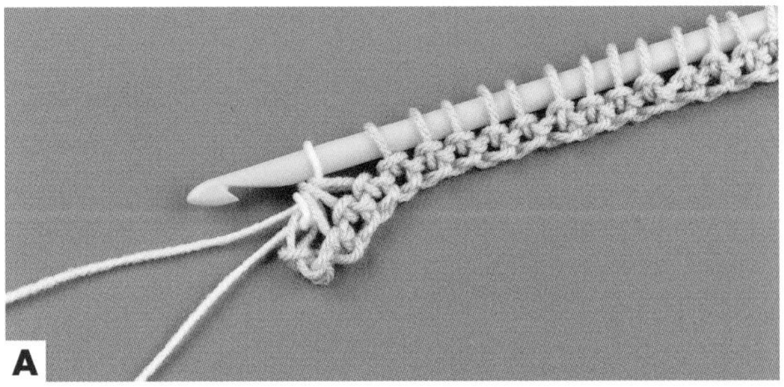

A

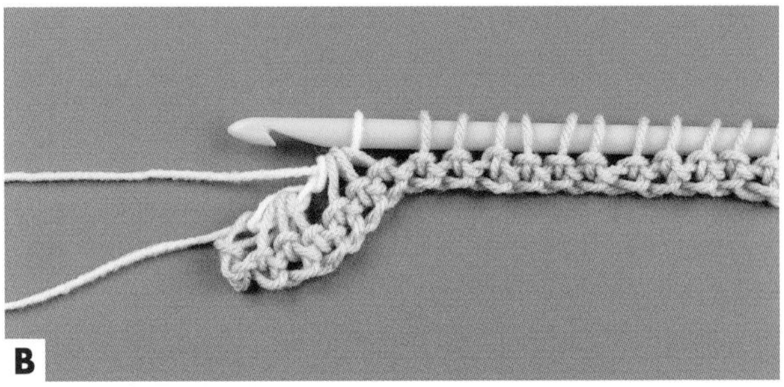

B

Row 3: Ch 1, sk first shell, pull up lp in first ch of next ch-3, insert hook in ch directly below on row 1, yo, pull through, ch 1, pull up lp in last ch of same ch-3 *(this completes a corn st—see Photo C)*, *sk next shell, pull up lp in first ch of next ch-3, insert hook in ch directly below on row 1, yo, pull through, ch 1, pull up lp in last ch of same ch-3 *(this completes a corn st)*, rep from * 31 times, sk last shell, pull up lp in last ch, turn. *(101 lps on hook)*

Row 4: With warm brown, yo, pull through one lp on hook, *ch 2, yo, pull through 4 lps on hook *(this completes a ch-3 and a shell)*, rep from * 32 times, ch 2, yo, pull through 2 lps on hook *(this completes a ch-3)*, **do not turn.**

Row 5: Ch 1, **corn st** *(see Special Stitch)*, [sk next shell on this row, corn st] 33 times, turn. *(103 lps on hook)*

Row 6: With yellow, yo, pull through 1 lp on hook, yo, pull through 4 lps on hook *(this completes a ch-1 and a shell)*, *ch 2, yo, pull through 4 lps on hook *(this completes a ch-3 and a shell)*, rep from * across, do not turn.

Row 7: Ch 1, sk first shell on this row, corn st, [sk next shell on this row, corn st] 32 times, sk last shell on this row, pull up lp in last ch, turn. *(101 lps on hook)*

Rows 8–76: [Rep rows 4–7 consecutively] 18 times, ending last rep with row 4.

Row 77: Ch 1, sl st in first ch of next ch-3, insert hook under top strand of 2 horizontal bars above first shell 3 rows below, yo, pull through, yo, pull through 2 lps on hook, sl st in last ch of same ch-3, [sk next shell on this row, sl st in first ch of next ch-3, insert hook under top strand of 2 horizontal bars above next shell 3 rows below, yo, pull through, yo, pull through 2 lps on hook, sl st in last ch of same ch-3] across. Fasten off.

FRINGE

Cut 1 strand 9 inches long of each warm brown and yellow. Hold all strands tog, fold in half, insert hook in end of row, pull fold through, pull ends through fold. Pull to tighten. Trim ends.

Attach Fringe in end of each row across each short edge. ■

Purple Passion

DESIGN BY **CAROLYN CHRISTMAS**

SKILL LEVEL

INTERMEDIATE

FINISHED SIZE

11 x 48½ inches

MATERIALS

MEDIUM

- Medium (worsted) weight nubby novelty yarn:
  12 oz/600 yds/340g variegated purple
- Fine (sport) weight chenille yarn:
  3 oz/100 yds/85g purple
- Crochenit hook

GAUGE

2 sts = 1 inch; 3 rows = 1 inch

PATTERN NOTE

Read General Instructions on page 2 before beginning pattern.

SPECIAL STITCH

High stitch (high st): Insert hook in next st or vertical bar, yo, pull lp through, ch 1.

GENERAL INSTRUCTIONS

Pull up lp: Insert hook in designated lp, bar or st, yo, draw lp through leaving lp on hook.

When picking up lps: Leave all lps on hook unless otherwise stated.

Turn: Rotate hook 180 degrees and slide all lps to opposite end. Do not turn unless otherwise stated.

Work lps off hook when adding a new color: With new color, place slip knot on hook, pull slip knot through 1 lp on hook, [yo, pull through 2 lps on hook] across.

Last lp remaining on hook at end of row is first vertical bar of new row.

Work lps off hook with a color already in use: Pick up color from row below, yo, pull through one lp on hook, [yo, pull through 2 lps on hook] across.

To end a color that is no longer needed: Work across the row as stated and cut yarn, leaving long end; secure the end temporarily by tying to an adjacent yarn end, or permanently by weaving back through an inch or so on the row before.

INSTRUCTIONS

WRAP

Row 1: Read General Instructions beg, with nubby yarn, ch 98, pull up lp in 3rd ch from hook, ch 1 *(high st)*, **high st** *(see Special Stitch)* in each ch across, turn. *(97 lps on hook)*

Row 2: With chenille yarn, work lps off hook, **do not turn**.

Row 3: Sk first vertical bar, pull up lp in each vertical bar across, turn.

Row 4: With nubby yarn, work lps off hook, **do not turn**.

Row 5: Ch 1, sk first vertical bar, high st in each vertical bar across, turn.

Rows 6–32: [Rep rows 2–5 consecutively] 7 times, ending last rep with row 4.

Row 33: To bind off, ch 1, skip first vertical bar, [high st in next vertical bar, yo, pull through 2 lps on hook] across. Fasten off.

KNOTTED FRINGE

For each Fringe, cut 3 strands nubby yarn, each 20 inches long. Holding all strands tog, fold in half, insert hook in end of row, pull fold through, pull all loose ends through fold. Pull to tighten. Trim.

Attach 9 Fringe evenly spaced across each short edge.

2ND ROW

Tie 3 strands from next 2 Fringes tog $1\frac{1}{2}$ inch from last knot *(see Fig. 1)* across. ■

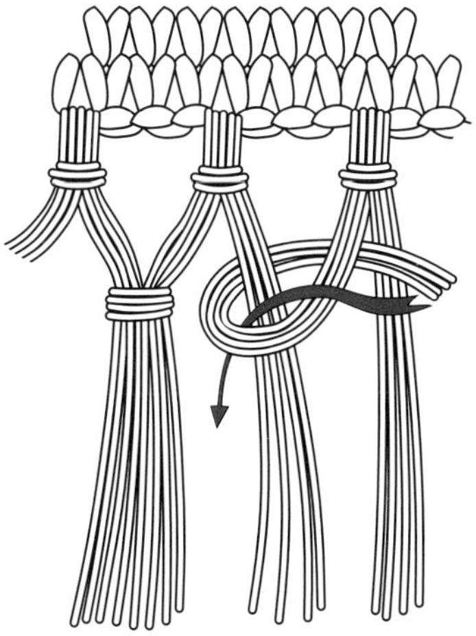

Fig. 1
Double Knot Fringe

Teal Treasure Afghan

DESIGN BY **CAROLYN CHRISTMAS**

SKILL LEVEL

INTERMEDIATE

FINISHED SIZE

42 inches square

MATERIALS

- Medium (worsted) weight yarn: 11 oz/550 yds/312g each dark teal and medium teal
- Size K/10½/6.5mm crochet hook
- Crochenit hook

4 MEDIUM

GAUGE

1 shell = 1 inch; 6 rows = 1½ inches

PATTERN NOTES

Read General Instructions on page 2 before beginning pattern.

Chain-3 at beginning of rows or rounds counts as first double crochet unless otherwise stated.

Join with slip stitch as indicated unless otherwise stated.

SPECIAL STITCH

Double crochet group (dc group): 3 dc in place indicated.

INSTRUCTIONS

AFGHAN

Row 1: With Crochenit hook and dark teal, ch 112, pull up lp in 2nd ch from hook, pull up lp in each ch across, turn. *(112 lps on hook)*

Row 2: To work lps off hook, with medium teal, pull through 1 lp on hook, [ch 2, yo, pull through 4 lps on hook *(counts as ch-3 and shell)*, rep from * across, **do not turn**.

Row 3: Ch 1, sk shells, pull up lp in each ch across, turn. *(112 lps on hook)*

Row 4: Rep row 2.

Row 5: Ch 1, sk shells, pull up lp in each ch across, turn.

Rows 6–152: [Rep rows 2–5 consecutively] 37 times, ending last rep with row 4. At end of last row, fasten off both colors.

BORDER

Rnd 1: Working around outer edge, with size K hook and dark teal, **join** *(see Pattern Notes)* in first ch sp of last row, **ch 3** *(see Pattern Notes)*, (2 dc, ch 2, 3 dc) in same ch sp *(corner)*, **dc group** *(see Special Stitch)* in each ch sp across to last ch sp, (3 dc, ch 2, 3 dc) in last ch sp, evenly sp 35 dc groups across ends of rows, working in sps between shells on opposite side of row 1, (3 dc, ch 2, 3 dc) in first sp, work dc group in each sp across to last sp, (3 dc, ch 2, 3 dc) in last sp, evenly sp 35 dc groups across ends of rows, join in 3rd ch of beg ch-3. Fasten off.

Rnd 2: Join medium teal with sc in first corner ch sp, ch 2, sc in same sp, ch 3, [sc in center st of next dc group, ch 3] across to next corner ch sp, *(sc, ch 2, sc) in next corner ch sp, ch 3, [sc in center st of next dc group, ch 3] across to next corner ch sp, rep from * around, join in beg sc. Fasten off.

Rnd 3: Join dark teal with sc in first corner ch sp, (2 dc, ch 2, 2 dc) in next ch sp, [sc in next ch sp, (2 dc, ch 2, 2 dc) in next ch sp] around, join in beg sc. Fasten off. ■

Morning Dew Lapghan

DESIGN BY **CAROLYN CHRISTMAS**

SKILL LEVEL

INTERMEDIATE

FINISHED SIZE
46 inches square

MATERIALS
- Red Heart Super Saver medium (worsted) weight yarn (7 oz/ 364 yds/198g per skein):
  2 skeins each #661 frosty green and #406 medium thyme
- Crochenit cable hook
- Size K/10½/6.5mm crochet hook

4 MEDIUM

GAUGE
With Crochenit hook: 4 high sts = 1½ inches; 9 rows = 2½ inches

PATTERN NOTES
Read General Instructions on page 2 before beginning pattern.

Fasten off colors when no longer needed.

Use Crochenit hook throughout unless otherwise stated.

Join with slip stitch as indicated unless otherwise stated.

SPECIAL STITCHES
High stitch (high st): Insert hook in place indicated, yo, pull through, ch 1.

Picot: Ch 3, sc in 3rd ch from hook.

INSTRUCTIONS
Row 1: With medium thyme, ch 113, pull up lp in 2nd ch from hook, pull up lp in each ch across, turn. *(113 lps on hook)*

Row 2: With frosty green, work lps off hook, **do not turn.**

Row 3: Ch 1, **high st** *(see Special Stitches)* in top 2 strands of each horizontal bar across, high st in last vertical bar, turn. *(113 lps on hook)*

Row 4: With medium thyme, pull through 1 lp on hook, ch 1, yo, pull through 4 lps on hook *(ch-2 and shell)*, *ch 2, yo, pull through 4 lps on hook *(ch-3 and shell)*, rep from * 35 times, ch 1, yo, pull through 2 lps on hook, **do not turn.**

Row 5: Ch 1, pull up lp in each ch across, turn. *(113 lps on hook)*

Rows 6–153: [Rep rows 2–5 consecutively] 37 times. At end of last row, **do not turn.**

Row 154: Work lps off hook. Fasten off.

BORDER
Rnd 1: With size K hook and frosty green, join with sc in first st, ch 2 *(corner)*, sc in same st, working in sps between bars, ch 1, sk first sp, sc in next sp, [ch 1, sk next sp, sc in next sp] 54 times, ch 1, sk last sp, (sc, ch 2, sc) in last st *(corner)*, evenly sp, (ch 1, sc) 55 times across ends of rows, working in starting ch on opposite side of row 1, ch 1, (sc, ch 2, sc) in first ch *(corner)*, [ch 1, sk next ch, sc in next sp] 55 times, ch 1, sk next ch, (sc, ch 2, sc) in last ch *(corner)*, evenly sp (ch 1, sc) 55 times across ends of rows, ch 1, **join** *(see Pattern Notes)* in beg sc. Fasten off.

Rnd 2: Join medium thyme in any corner ch sp, ch 5, dc in same ch sp, ch 1, [dc in next ch sp, ch 1] across to next corner ch sp, *(dc, ch 2, dc) in corner ch sp, ch 1, [dc in next ch sp, ch 1] across to next corner ch sp, rep from * around, join in 3rd ch of ch-5.

Rnd 3: Ch 1, sc in first st, **picot** *(see Special Stitches)*, (2 dc, picot) twice in each corner ch sp with (sc, picot) in each st around, join in beg sc. Fasten off. ■

Lovely BABY

DESIGN BY **MARY MIDDLETON**

SKILL LEVEL

INTERMEDIATE

FINISHED SIZE

32 x 36 inches

MATERIALS

- Medium (worsted) weight yarn: 8 oz/400 yds/227g each white and blue
- Crochenit hook or cable hook
- Stitch markers

GAUGE

3 sts = 1 inch; 18 rows = 3 inches

PATTERN NOTES

Read General Instructions on page 2 before beginning pattern.

Fasten off colors when no longer needed.

SPECIAL STITCH

High stitch (high st): Insert hook in next vertical bar or st indicated, yo, pull lp through, ch 1.

INSTRUCTIONS

AFGHAN

Row 1: With blue, ch 90, pull up lp in 2nd ch from hook, pull up lp in each ch across, turn. *(90 lps on hook)*

Row 2: With white, work lps off hook, **do not turn**.

Row 3: Ch 1, pull up lp in top strand of first **horizontal bar** (*see Fig. 1*), insert hook under next 2 vertical bars at same time, yo, pull up lp, [pull up lp in top strand of next horizontal bar, insert hook under next 2 vertical bars at same time, yo, pull up lp] across to last horizontal bar, pull up lp in top strand of last horizontal bar, turn.

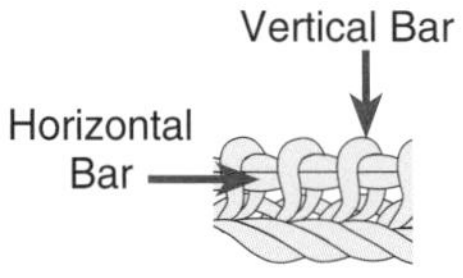

Fig. 1

Row 4: With blue, work lps off hook, do not turn.

Row 5: Rep row 3.

Rows 6–148: [Rep rows 2–5 consecutively] 36 times, ending last rep with row 4.

Row 149: Ch 1, sl st in top strand of first horizontal bar, sl st under next two vertical bars at same time, [sl st in top strand of next horizontal bar, sl st under next 2 vertical bars at same time] across to last horizontal bar, sl st in top strand of last horizontal bar. Fasten off.

EDGING

Rnd 1: Join blue with sc in first st, working around outer edge in sts and in ends of rows, evenly spacing sts so piece lies flat, sc around, join with sl st in beg sc, turn. Fasten off.

Rnd 2: Working this rnd in **front lps** *(see Stitch Guide)* and leaving lps on hook as you work, work rnd 2 in the following steps:

A. Make slip knot with white, pull slip knot through first st at 1 corner, ch 1, **high st** *(see Special Stitch)* in same st, 2 high sts in next st, high st in each st across to 2 sts before next corner, 2 high sts in each of next 4 sts, *(2 increases on each side of corner, mark center of corner)*, high st in each of next 5 sts, turn;

B. With blue, work lps off to last 5 lps, drop blue, turn;

C. With white, continue to work high st across to 2 sts before next corner, 2 high sts in each of next 4 sts, *(mark center of corner)*, high st in each of next 5 sts, turn, drop white;

D. Rep step B;

E & F. Rep steps C and B;

G. With white, continue to work high st across to last 2 sts before first corner, 2 high sts in each of last 2 sts *(mark center of corner)*, turn;

H. With blue, work rem lps off hook;

I. Ch 1, drop lp from hook, insert hook through first ch and vertical bar, pull dropped lp through, **do not turn**. Fasten off white.

Rnd 3: Work rnd 3 in the following steps:

A. Ch 1 with blue, *(counts as first high st)*, 2 high sts in top strand of next 2 horizontal bars, high st in top strand of each horizontal bar across to 2 horizontal bars before next marked corner, 2 high sts in top strand of next 5 horizontal bars *(mark center of corner)*, high st in top strand of each of next 5 horizontal bars, drop blue, turn;

B. With white, work lps off to last 5 lps, drop white, turn;

C. With blue, continue to work high st in each horizontal bar across to 2 horizontal bars before next marked corner, 2 high sts in top strand of each of next 5 horizontal bars *(mark center of corner)*, high st in top strand of each of next 5 horizontal bars, turn, drop blue;

D. Rep step B;

E & F. Rep steps C and B;

G. With blue, continue to work high st in top strand of each horizontal bar across to 2 horizontal bars before first corner, 2 high sts in top strand of each of last 2 horizontal bars, high st in same ch as joining st of last rnd, *(mark center of corner)*, turn;

H. With white, work rem lps off hook;

I. Ch 1, drop lp from hook, insert hook through first ch and vertical bar, pull dropped lp through, do not turn. Fasten off blue.

Rnd 4: Work rnd 4 in the following steps:

A. Ch 1 with white, *(counts as first high st)*, 2 high sts in top strand of each of next 2 horizontal bars, high st in top strand of each horizontal bar across to 2 horizontal bars before next marked corner, 2 high sts in top strand of each of next 5 horizontal bars *(mark center of corner)*, high st in top strand of each of next 5 horizontal bars, drop white, turn;

B. With blue, yo, pull through 2 lps on hook, *ch 1, yo, pull through 3 lps on hook, *(ch-2, and shell made)*, rep from * across to last 4 or 5 lps, drop blue, turn;

C. With white, continue to work high st in each horizontal bar across to 2 horizontal bars before next marked corner, 2 high sts in top strand of each of next 5 horizontal bars, high st in top strand of each of next 5 horizontal bars, drop white, turn;

D. With blue, [ch 1, yo, pull through 3 lps on hook] across to last 4 or 5 sts, drop blue, turn;

E & F. Rep steps C and D;

G. With white, continue to work high st in top strand of each horizontal bar across to 2 horizontal bars before first corner, high st number of times it takes in top strand of each of next 2 horizontal bars to make sure you have enough sts to work the sts off in multiples of 2, turn;

H. With blue, [ch 1, yo, pull through 3 lps on hook] across, ch 1, drop lp from hook, insert hook in top of first shell, pull dropped lp through, **do not turn**. Fasten off.

Rnd 5: Join blue with sl st in top of any shell, ch 1, [sl st in top of next shell, ch 1] around, join with sl st in beg sl st. Fasten off. ■

Pretty Pink

DESIGN BY **MARY MIDDLETON**

SKILL LEVEL

INTERMEDIATE

FINISHED SIZE

33 x 35 inches

MATERIALS

- Medium (worsted) weight yarn: 7 oz/350 yds/198g each pink and white
- Crochenit hook or cable hook
- Stitch markers

GAUGE

3 sts = 2½ inches; 4 rows = 1 inch

PATTERN NOTES

Read General Instructions on page 2 before beginning pattern.

Fasten off colors when no longer needed.

SPECIAL STITCH

High stitch (high st): Insert hook in next vertical bar or st indicated, yo, pull lp through, ch 1.

INSTRUCTIONS

AFGHAN

Row 1: With pink, ch 82, pull up lp in 2nd ch from hook, pull up lp in each ch across, turn. *(82 lps on hook)*

Row 2: With white, work lps off hook, **do not turn**.

Row 3: Sk first vertical bar, pull up lp in each vertical bar across, turn.

Row 4: With pink, pull through first lp on hook, *ch 2, yo, pull through 4 lps on hook *(ch-3 and shell completed)*, rep from * across, **do not turn**.

Row 5: Ch 1, sk shells, pull up lp in each ch across, turn.

Rows 6–119: [Rep rows 2–5 consecutively] 29 times, ending last rep with row 3.

Row 120: With pink, work lps off hook, do not turn.

Row 121: Ch 1, sl st in each vertical bar across. Fasten off.

EDGING

Rnd 1: Now working in rnds, join white with sc in first st, working around outer edge in sts and in ends of rows, evenly spacing sts so piece lies flat, sc around, join with sl st in beg sc, **turn**.

Rnd 2: Working this rnd in **front lps** *(see Stitch Guide)* and leaving lps on hook as you work, work rnd 2 in the following steps:

A. Ch 1, **high st** *(see Special Stitch)* in same st, 2 high sts in next st, high st in each st across to 2 sts before next corner, 2 high sts in each of next 4 sts, *(2 increases on each side of corner, mark center of corner)*, high st in each of next 5 sts, turn;

B. With pink, work lps off to last 5 lps, drop pink, turn;

C. With white, continue to work high st across to 2 sts before next corner, 2 high sts in each of next 4 sts, *(mark center of corner)*, high st in each of next 5 sts, turn, drop white;

D. Rep step B;

E & F. Rep steps C and B;

G. With white, continue to work high st across to last 2 sts before first corner, 2 high sts in each of last 2 sts *(mark center of corner)*, turn;

H. With pink, work rem lps off hook;

I. Ch 1, drop lp from hook, insert hook through first ch and vertical bar, pull dropped lp through, do not turn. Fasten off white.

Rnd 3: Work rnd 3 in the following steps:

A. Ch 1 with pink, *(counts as first high st)*, 2 high sts in top strand of each of next 2 horizontal bars, high st in top strand of each horizontal bar across to 2 horizontal bars before next marked corner, 2 high sts in top strand of each of next 5 horizontal bars *(mark center of corner)*, high st in top strand of each of next 5 horizontal bars, drop pink, turn;

B. With white, work lps off to last 5 lps, drop white, turn;

C. With pink, continue to work high st in each horizontal bar across to 2 horizontal bars before next marked corner, 2 high sts in top strand of each of next 5 horizontal bars *(mark center of corner)*, high st in top strand of each of next 5 horizontal bars, turn, drop pink;

D. Rep step B;

E & F. Rep steps C and B;

G. With pink, continue to work high st in top strand of each horizontal bar across to 2 horizontal bars before first corner, 2 high sts in top strand of each of last 2 horizontal bars, high st in same ch as joining st of last rnd, *(mark center of corner)*, turn;

H. With white, work rem lps off hook;

I. Ch 1, drop lp from hook, insert hook through first ch and vertical bar, pull dropped lp through, do not turn. Fasten off pink.

Rnd 4: Work rnd 4 in the following steps:

A. Ch 1 with white, *(counts as first high st)*, 2 high sts in top strand of each of next 2 horizontal bars, high st in top strand of each horizontal bar across to 2 horizontal bars before next marked corner, 2 high sts in top strand of each of next 5 horizontal bars *(mark center of corner)*, high st in top strand of each of next 5 horizontal bars, drop white, turn;

B. With pink, yo, pull through 3 lps on hook, *ch 2, yo, pull through 4 lps on hook, *(ch-3 and shell completed)*, rep from * across to last 4 or 5 lps, drop pink, turn;

C. With white, continue to work high st in each horizontal bar across to 2 horizontal bars before next marked corner, 2 high sts in top strand of each of next 5 horizontal bars, high st in top strand of each of next 5 horizontal bars, drop white, turn;

D. With pink, [ch 2, yo, pull through 4 lps on hook] across to last 4 or 5 sts, drop pink, turn;

E & F. Rep steps C and D;

G. With white, continue to work high st in top strand of each horizontal bar across to 2 horizontal bars before first corner, high st number of times it takes in top strand of next 2 horizontal bars to make sure you have enough sts to work the sts off in multiples of 3, turn;

H. With pink, [ch 2, yo, pull through 4 lps on hook] across, ch 3, join with sl st in top of first shell. Fasten off.

Rnd 5: With RS facing, join white with sc in any shell, ch 3, [sc in next shell, ch 3] around, join with sl st in beg sc. Fasten off.

Rnd 6: Join pink with sc in center ch of any ch-3, ch 3, [sc in center ch of next ch-3, ch 3] around, join with sl st in beg sc. Fasten off. ■

Southwest Afghan

DESIGN BY **CAROLYN CHRISTMAS**

SKILL LEVEL

INTERMEDIATE

FINISHED SIZE
48 x 68 inches, excluding tassels

MATERIALS
- Bulky (chunky) weight yarn:
  26 oz/910 yds/737g each violet and silver
  7 oz/245 yds/198g black
- Crochenit hook or cable hook
- Size K/10½/6.5mm crochet hook

4 MEDIUM

GAUGE
Panel = 8 inches across

PATTERN NOTES
Read General Instructions on page 2 before beginning pattern.

Fasten off colors when no longer needed.

Use Crochenit hook throughout unless otherwise stated.

Join with slip stitch as indicated unless otherwise stated.

INSTRUCTIONS
AFGHAN
FIRST PANEL

Row 1: With silver, ch 149, pull up lp in 2nd ch from hook, pull up lp in each ch across, turn. *(149 lps on hook)*

Row 2: With violet, pull through first lp on hook, [ch 1, yo, pull through 4 lps on hook *(ch-2 and shell completed, see Photo A)*, ch 1, yo, pull through 2 lps on hook *(ch-2 and vertical bar completed, see Photo B)*] across, **do not turn.**

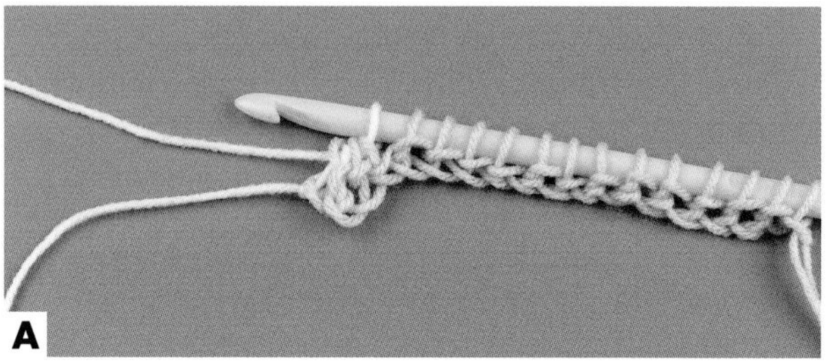
A

B

Row 3: Ch 1, [sk first ch of next ch-2, pull up lp in next ch, pull up lp in horizontal bar above next shell, pull up lp in next ch, pull up lp in next vertical bar] across, turn.

Row 4: With silver, pull through first lp on hook, [ch 1, yo, pull through 4 lps on hook *(ch-2 and shell completed)*, ch 1, yo, pull through 2 lps on hook *(ch-2 and vertical bar completed)*] across, do not turn.

Row 5: Ch 1, [sk first ch of next ch-2, pull up lp in next ch, pull up lp in horizontal bar above next shell, pull up lp in next ch, pull up lp in next vertical bar] across, turn.

Row 6: With violet, pull through first lp on hook, *ch 1, yo, pull through 4 lps on hook *(ch-2 and shell completed)*, ch 1, yo, pull through 2 lps on hook *(ch-2 and vertical bar completed)*, rep from * across. Fasten off.

Row 7: Working in starting ch on opposite side of row 1, with loose ends of silver on the right, pull up lp in each ch across, turn. *(149 lps on hook)*

Rows 8–12: Rep rows 2–6.

EDGING

Rnd 1: With violet, **join** *(see Pattern Notes)* in sp between rows 1 and 7 on 1 end, ch 4 *(counts as first tr)*, 8 tr in same sp, sc in next ch sp, [ch 1, sc in next ch sp] across, 9 tr in sp between rows 1 and 7 on other end of Panel, sc in next ch sp, [ch 1, sc in next ch sp] across, join in 4th ch of beg ch-4.

Rnd 2: Ch 4 *(counts as first dc and ch-1 sp)*, [dc in next tr, ch 1] 3 times, *(dc, ch 1) twice in next tr, [dc in next tr, ch 1] 4 times, [dc in next sc, ch 1] across to next end*, [dc in next tr, ch 1] 4 times, rep between *, join in 3rd ch of beg ch-4. Fasten off.

Rnd 3: Join black in 1 center end ch sp, (ch 3, dc, ch 1, 2 dc) in same ch sp, ch 1, (sc, ch 1) in each dc around to next end ch sp, (2 dc, ch 1, 2 dc) in end ch sp, ch 1, (sc, ch 1) in each dc across, join in 3rd ch of beg ch-3. Fasten off.

Rnd 4: Join silver in 1 end ch sp, (ch 3, dc, ch 1, 2 dc) in same ch sp, *[ch 1, dc in next ch sp] 3 times, ch 1, (dc, ch 1, dc) in next ch sp, ch 1, (dc, ch 1) in each ch sp across to 4 ch sps before next end ch sp, (dc, ch 1, dc) in next ch sp, ch 1, [dc in next ch sp, ch 1] 3 times*, (2 dc, ch 1, 2 dc) in next end ch sp, rep between *, join in 3rd ch of beg ch-3. Fasten off.

NEXT PANEL

Work same as First Panel.

EDGING

Rnds 1–3: Work rnds 1–3 of First Panel Edging.

Rnd 4: Join silver in 1 end ch sp, (ch 3, dc, ch 1, 2 dc) in same sp, [ch 1, dc in next ch sp] 3 times, ch 1, dc in next ch sp, joining to long edge of last Panel, sl st in corresponding ch sp on other Panel, dc in same ch sp on this Panel, [sl st in next ch sp on other Panel, dc in next ch sp on this Panel] across to 4 ch sps before next end ch sp, sl st in next ch sp on other Panel, dc in next ch sp on this Panel, sl st in next ch sp on other Panel, dc in same ch sp on this Panel, [ch 1, dc in next ch sp] 3 times, ch 1, (2 dc, ch 1, 2 dc) in next end ch sp, [ch 1, dc in next ch sp] 3 times, ch 1, (dc, ch 1, dc) in next ch sp, ch 1, (dc, ch 1) in each ch sp across to 4 ch sps before next end ch sp, (dc, ch 1, dc) in next ch sp, ch 1, [dc in next ch sp, ch 1] 3 times, join in 3rd ch of beg ch-3. Fasten off.

Work Next Panel 4 times for a total of 6 Panels.

TASSEL
MAKE 12.

Cut 20 strands violet, each 18 inches long. Tie separate strand violet tightly around middle of all strands, fold strands in half. Wrap another strand black around strands 2 inches from top of fold, covering ½ inch. Secure and hide ends inside Tassel. Trim all ends evenly.

Tie 1 Tassel to each end of each Panel. ■

Cozy Slippers

SKILL LEVEL

BEGINNER

FINISHED SIZE

One size fits most adults

MATERIALS

- Lion Brand Jiffy bulky (chunky) weight yarn (3 oz/135 yds/85g per ball):
  2 balls each #106 baby blue and #100 white
- Size K/10½/6.5mm crochet hook
- Crochenit cable hook
- Tapestry needle
- 1½-inch square piece of cardboard

5 BULKY

GAUGE

With Crochenit hook: 5 sts = 2 inches, 14 rows = 2 inches

PATTERN NOTES

Read General Instructions on page 2 before beginning pattern.

Here's a good rule of thumb to help you remember when to turn the hook. If you have loops on the hook, it's time to turn and change colors. If you have only one loop on the hook at the end of a row, do not turn, work next row with the same color you're working with.

Fasten off colors when no longer needed.

Use Crochenit hook throughout unless otherwise stated.

Join with slip stitch as indicated unless otherwise stated.

INSTRUCTIONS

SLIPPER

MAKE 2.

Row 1: With Crochenit hook and baby blue, ch 44, working in **back lps** *(see Stitch Guide)* only, insert hook in 2nd ch from hook, yo, pull lp through *(see Photo A)* leaving lp on hook, * insert hook in back lp of next ch, yo, pull lp through, rep from * across *(see Photo B)* leaving all lps on hook, drop blue but do not fasten off.

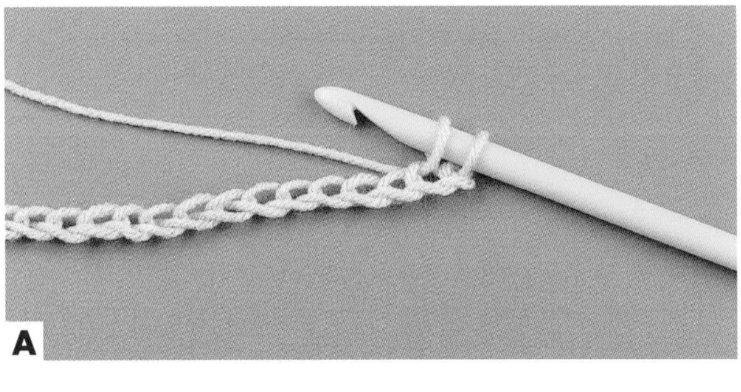

A

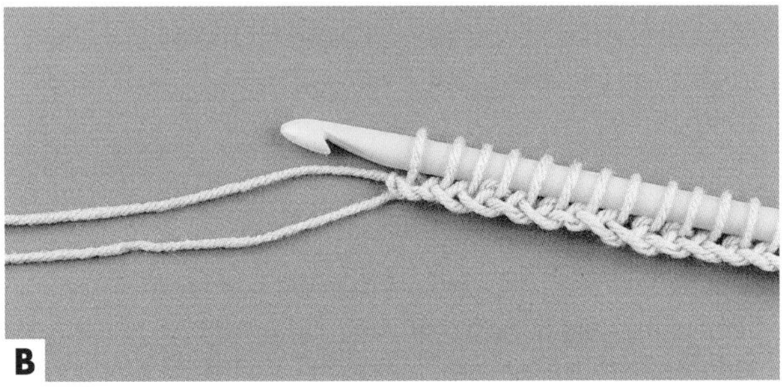

B

When working the Basic Stitch, at this point you will have the same number of lps as your original ch. In this case, you will have 44 lps on the hook. Each of these lps counts as a stitch, and in the next row, each lp will be referred to as a vertical bar.

Row 2: To work lps off hook, make a slip knot with white, place slip knot on hook, pull slip knot through first lp on hook *(pulling the slip knot through the first lp makes the first stitch of the row)*, yo, pull through next 2 lps on hook *(when you pull through the next 2 lps on hook in this step, you will pull through 1 lp of each color)*, [yo, pull through next 2 lps on hook] across, leaving last lp on hook, do not turn hook at end of this row. Continue working with white.

Row 3: Sk first vertical bar, insert hook under next vertical bar, yo and pull up lp, pull up lp in each vertical bar across, drop white yarn but do not cut. Turn hook.

Row 4: Pick up blue, yo and pull through first lp on hook, yo, [pull through next 2 lps on hook] across, **do not turn**.

Row 5: Sk first vertical bar, pull up lp in next vertical bar, pull up lp in each vertical bar across, drop blue, turn hook.

Row 6: With white, rep row 4.

Row 7: Continuing with white, rep row 5.

Rows 8–27: [Rep rows 4–7 consecutively] 5 times.

Row 28: With blue, rep row 4, do not turn hook. Fasten off both colors.

FOOT

Row 29: With blue, insert hook under 11th vertical bar from right-hand side of work, pull up lp, pull up lp in each of next 23 vertical bars *(24 lps on hook)*, leaving last 10 vertical bars unworked, drop blue but do not cut. Turn hook.

Row 30: Place white slip knot on hook, pull slip knot through 1 lp on hook, [yo, pull through 2 lps on hook] across, **do not turn**.

Row 31: Rep row 5. *(24 lps on hook)*

Next rows: Rep rows 4–7 consecutively until piece is as long as foot, ending with row 4 or 6. At end of last row, leaving long end for weaving, fasten off.

Weave end through sts of last row, pull to gather, secure.

Sew from toe to cuff for instep. Sew from heel to top of cuff to form back seam.

EDGING

With size K crochet hook and blue, working around top and sides of cuff, join with sc in any sp between vertical bars on last row, sc in each sp between vertical bars on last row and in end of each color section around cuff, **join** *(see Pattern Notes)* in beg sc. Fasten off.

POMPOM
MAKE 2.

Wrap white around cardboard 35 times, slide lps off cardboard, tie separate strand white around middle of all lps. Cut lps. Trim ends.

TIE

With size K crochet hook and blue, ch 55. Fasten off.

Tack 1 Pompom to each end of Tie.

Tack center of Tie to center front of Slipper at bottom of Cuff as shown in photo. Tie ends into a bow. ■

Corn Stitch Table Runner

SKILL LEVEL

INTERMEDIATE

FINISHED SIZE
16 x 39 inches

MATERIALS

- Lily Sugar'n Cream Cotton medium (worsted) weight cotton yarn ($2\frac{1}{2}$ oz/120 yds/70g per ball):
  2 balls each #00082 jute and #00004 ecru
- Size K/$10\frac{1}{2}$/6.5mm crochet hook
- Crochenit hook or cable hook

4 MEDIUM

GAUGE
With Crochenit hook: 3 corn sts = $4\frac{1}{4}$ inches; 7 rows = 2 inches

PATTERN NOTES
Read General Instructions on page 2 before beginning pattern.

Fasten off colors when no longer needed.

Use Crochenit hook throughout unless otherwise stated.

Join with slip stitch as indicated unless otherwise stated.

SPECIAL STITCH
Corn stitch (corn st): Pull up lp in first ch of next ch-3, insert hook under top strand of 2 horizontal bars above next shell 3 rows below, yo, pull through, ch 1, pull up lp in last ch of same ch-3.

INSTRUCTIONS
TABLE RUNNER
Row 1: With jute, ch 43, pull up lp in 2nd ch from hook, pull up lp in each ch across, turn. *(43 lps on hook)*

Row 2: With ecru, yo, pull through 1 lp on hook, yo, pull through 4 lps on hook *(this completes a ch-1 and a shell—see Photo A)*, *ch 2, yo, pull through 4 lps on hook *(this completes a ch-3 and a shell—see Photo B)*, rep from * across, **do not turn**.

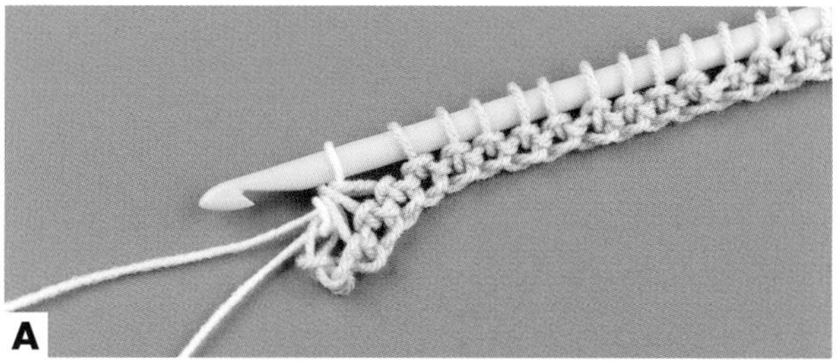
A

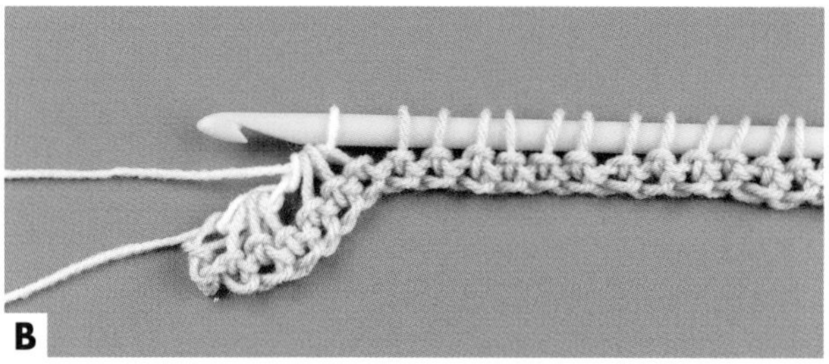
B

Row 3: Ch 1, sk first shell, pull up lp in first ch of next ch-3, insert hook in ch directly below on row 1, yo, pull through, ch 1, pull up lp in last ch of same ch-3 *(this completes a corn st—see Photo C)*, *sk next shell, pull up lp in first ch of next ch-3, insert hook in ch directly below on row 1, yo, pull through, ch 1, pull up lp in last ch of same ch-3 *(this completes a corn st)*, rep from * 11 times, sk last shell, pull up lp in last ch, turn. *(41 lps on hook)*

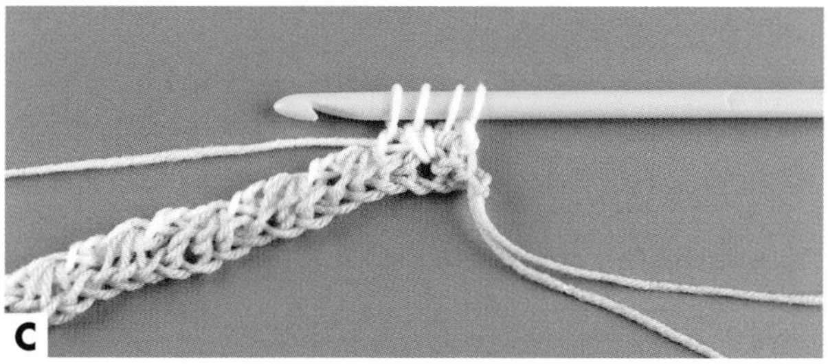
C

Row 4: With jute, yo, pull through 1 lp on hook, *ch 2, yo, pull through 4 lps on hook *(this completes a ch-3 and a shell)*, rep from * 12 times, ch 2, yo, pull through 2 lps on hook *(this completes a ch-3)*, do not turn.

Row 5: Ch 1, **corn st** *(see Special Stitch)*, [sk next shell on this row, corn st] across, turn. *(43 lps on hook)*

Row 6: With ecru, yo, pull through 1 lp on hook, yo, pull through 4 lps on hook *(this completes a ch-1 and a shell)*, *ch 2, yo, pull through 4 lps on hook *(this completes a ch-3 and a shell)*, rep from * across, do not turn.

Row 7: Ch 1, sk first shell, corn st, [sk next shell on this row, corn st] 12 times, sk last shell on this row, pull up lp in last ch, turn. *(41 lps on hook)*

Rows 8–196: [Rep rows 4–7 consecutively] 48 times, ending last rep with row 4.

Row 197: To bind off, ch 1, sl st in first ch of next ch-3, insert hook under top strand of 2 horizontal bars above first shell 3 rows below, yo, pull through, yo, pull through 2 lps on hook, sl st in last ch of same ch-3, [sk next shell on this row, sl st in first ch of next ch-3, insert hook under top strand of 2 horizontal bars above next shell 3 rows below, yo, pull through, yo, pull through 2 lps on hook, sl st in last ch of same ch-3] across. Fasten off.

EDGING

Working around outer edge, with K hook, **join** *(see Pattern Notes)* ecru in first st of last row, ch 3 *(counts as first dc)*, 4 dc in same st, sk next st, sc in next st, 2 dc in next st above shell, sc in next st, [sk next st, 2 dc in next st, sc in next st] across to last st, 5 dc in last st, working in ends of rows, sc in first ecru row, [easing to fit so piece lies flat, work 2 dc in end of next colored section, sc in end of next colored section] across, working in starting on opposite side of row 1, 5 dc in first ch, [sk next ch, sc in next ch, 2 dc in next ch] across to last 3 chs, sk next ch, sc in next ch, 5 dc in last ch, working in ends of rows, sc in first ecru row, [easing to fit so piece lies flat, 2 dc in end of next colored section, sc in end of next colored section] around, join in 3rd ch of beg ch-3. Fasten off. ■

Lacy Stole

DESIGN BY **MARY MIDDLETON**

SKILL LEVEL

INTERMEDIATE

FINISHED SIZE

17 x 60 inches, excluding Fringe

MATERIALS

MEDIUM 4

- Medium (worsted) weight yarn: 8 oz/400 yds/227g white
- Size 10 crochet cotton: 300 yds white/gold metallic
- Crochenit hook or cable hook

GAUGE

3 very fancy sts = 2 inches; 4 rows 1½ inches

PATTERN NOTES

Read General Instructions on page 2 before beginning pattern.

Fasten off colors when no longer needed.

Yarn side is right side of work.

SPECIAL STITCHES

High stitch (high st): Insert hook in next vertical bar or st indicated, yo, pull lp through, ch 1.

Very fancy stitch (very fancy st): Yo, insert hook in next 2 vertical bars at same time, yo, pull lp through, ch 1.

INSTRUCTIONS

STOLE

Row 1: With yarn, ch 49, pull up lp in 3rd ch from hook, ch 1 *(high st)*, **high st** *(see Special Stitches)* in each ch across, turn. *(48 lps on hook)*

Row 2: With thread, work lps off hook, **do not turn**.

Row 3: Ch 1, sk first vertical bar, **very fancy st** *(see Special Stitches)* across to last vertical bar, high st in last vertical bar, turn.

Row 4: With yarn, work lps off hook, do not turn.

Row 5: Ch 1, sk first vertical bar, very fancy st across to last vertical bar, high st in last vertical bar, turn.

Rows 6–160: [Rep rows 2–5 consecutively] 39 times, ending last rep with row 4.

Row 161: Ch 1, sc in first vertical bar, [2 sc in next 2 vertical bars at same time] across to last vertical bar, sc in last vertical bar. Fasten off. *(48 sc)*

FIRST SIDE TRIM

Row 1: Join yarn with sc in end of row 161, evenly sp 113 more sc in ends of rows across, ending at row 1, **do not turn**. Fasten off.

Row 2: Join thread with sc in first st, sc in each st across. Fasten off.

2ND SIDE TRIM

Row 1: Join yarn with sc in end of row 1 on other side of Stole, evenly sp 113 more sc in ends of rows across, ending at row 161, **do not turn**. Fasten off.

Row 2: Join thread with sc in first st, sc in each st across. Fasten off.

FRINGE

For each corner Fringe, cut 3 strands of yarn and 2 strands of thread, each 12 inches long, holding all strands tog, fold in half, insert hook in st at corner, pull fold through, pull all loose ends through fold. Pull to tighten. Trim ends.

For each center Fringe, cut 2 strands of yarn and 1 strand of thread, each 12 inches long, holding all strands tog, fold in half, insert hook in st, pull fold through, pull all loose ends through fold. Pull to tighten. Trim ends.

Attach 1 corner Fringe in each corner and evenly sp 23 center Fringe in sts between corners on short ends of Stole. ■

Comfort **Slippers**

DESIGN BY **DARLA HASSELL**

SKILL LEVEL

INTERMEDIATE

FINISHED SIZE

Fits up to 12-inch sole

MATERIALS

- Red Heart Super Saver medium (worsted) weight yarn (7 oz/ 364 yds/198g per skein):
  1 skein each #776 dark orchid and #528 medium purple
- Crochenit cable hook
- Tapestry needle

GAUGE

Heel pattern: 7 sts = 2 inches; 4 rows = 1 inch

Toe pattern: 3 corn sts = 3¼ inches; 4 rows = 1 inch

PATTERN NOTES

Read General Instructions on page 2 before beginning pattern.

Fasten off colors when no longer needed.

Join with slip stitch as indicated unless otherwise stated.

SPECIAL STITCHES

Corn stitch (corn st): Pull up lp in first ch of next ch-3, insert hook under top strand of 2 horizontal bars above next shell 3 rows below, yo, pull through, ch 1, pull up lp in last ch of same ch-3.

Cluster (cl): Holding back last lp of each st on hook, 2 dc in place indicated, yo, pull through all lps on hook.

INSTRUCTIONS

SLIPPER

MAKE 2.

Row 1: Starting at heel, with dark orchid, ch 40, pull up lp in 2nd ch from hook, pull up lp in each ch across, turn. *(40 lps on hook)*

Row 2: With medium purple, work lps off hook, **do not turn.**

Row 3: Ch 1, sk first vertical bar, pull up lp in each **horizontal bar** *(see Fig. 1)* across, turn.

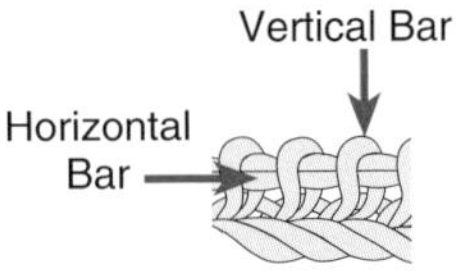

Fig. 1

Row 4: With dark orchid, work lps off hook, **do not turn**.

Row 5: Ch 1, sk first vertical bar, pull up lp in each horizontal bar across, turn.

Rows 6–22: [Rep rows 2–5 consecutively] 5 times, ending last rep with row 2.

Row 23: Ch 1, sk first vertical bar, sl st in each horizontal bar across, turn. Fasten off both colors.

TOE

Row 24: Sk first 8 sts, join dark orchid with sc in next st, sc in each of next 21 sts, leaving rem sts unworked, turn. *(22 sc)*

Row 25: Ch 1, sk first st, pull up lp in **front lp** *(see Stitch Guide)* only of each st across, turn. *(22 lps on hook)*

Row 26: With medium purple, pull through first lp on hook, yo, pull through 4 lps on hook *(this completes a ch-1 and a shell—see Photo A)*, *ch 2, yo, pull through 4 lps on hook *(this completes a ch-3 and a shell—see Photo B)*, rep from * across, do not turn.

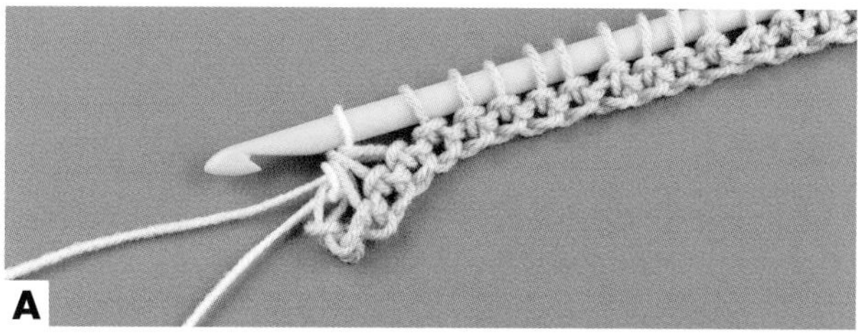
A

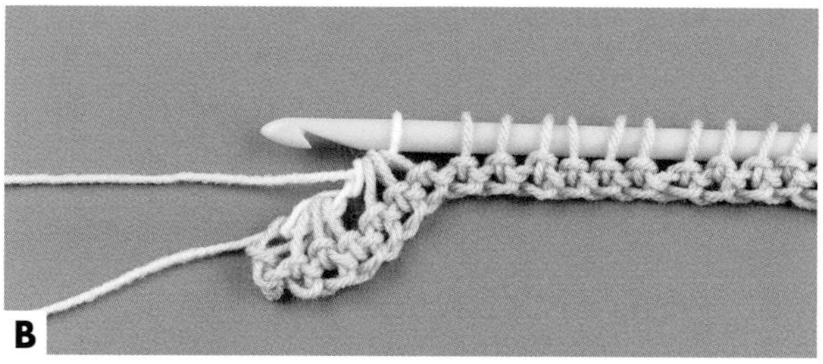
B

Row 27: Ch 1, sk first shell, pull up lp in first ch of next ch-3, insert hook in st directly below on row before last, yo, pull lp through, ch 1, pull up lp in last ch of same ch-3 *(this completes a corn st—see Photo C)*, *sk next shell, pull up lp in first ch of next ch-3, insert hook in st directly below on row before last, yo, pull lp through, ch 1, pull up lp in last ch of same ch-3 *(this completes a corn st)*, rep from * across to last shell, sk last shell, pull up lp in last ch, turn. *(20 lps on hook)*

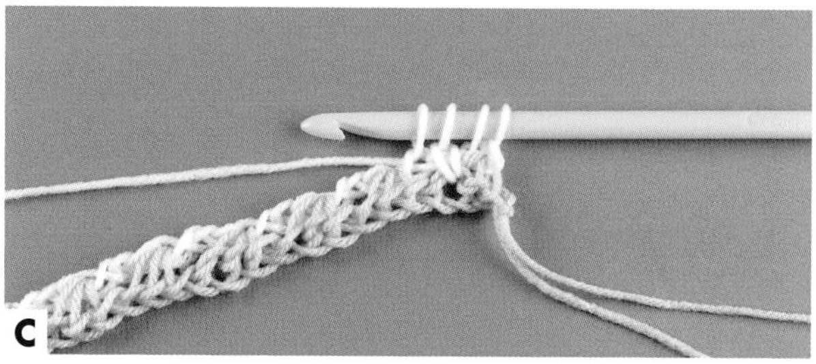
C

Row 28: With dark orchid, yo, pull through first lp on hook, *ch 2, yo, pull through 4 lps on hook *(this completes a ch-3 and a shell)*, rep from * across to last 2 lps on hook, ch 2, yo, pull through last 2 lps on hook *(this completes a ch-3)*, do not turn.

Row 29: Ch 1, **corn st** *(see Special Stitches)*, [sk next shell on last row, corn st] across, turn.

Row 30: With medium purple, yo, pull through first lp on hook, yo, pull through 4 lps on hook *(this completes a ch-1 and a shell)*, *ch 2, yo, pull through 4 lps on hook *(this completes a ch-3 and a shell)*, rep from * across, do not turn.

Row 31: Ch 1, sk first shell, corn st, sk next shell on last row, [corn st, sk next shell on last row] across to last ch, pull up lp in last ch, turn.

Rows 32–40: [Rep rows 28–31 consecutively] 3 times, ending last rep with row 28. At end of last row, fasten off medium purple. Leaving long end for sewing, fasten off dark orchid.

Weave long end through sts of last row, pull tight to gather Toe, secure, sew ends of rows 24–40 tog.

For heel seam, fold row 1 in half, sew starting ch tog.

CUFF TRIM

Row 1: Working in ends of rows across top of Slipper, join dark orchid with sc in end of first row, evenly sp 18 more sc across, do not turn. Fasten off. *(19 sc)*

Row 2: Join *(see Pattern Notes)* dark orchid in first st, (ch 2, dc) in same st *(counts as first cl)*, *ch 1, sk next st, **cl** *(see Special Stitches)* in next st, rep from * across. Fasten off.

Rnd 3: Join medium purple in first st on row 1, ch 6 *(counts as first dc and ch-3)*, dc in same st, (dc, ch 3, dc) in each ch sp across, (dc, ch 3 dc) in last st on row 1 *(same st as last cl on last row)*. Fasten off.

DRAWSTRING

With 2 strands dark orchid held tog, ch 60. Fasten off.

Weave drawstring through sps between sts of row, 1 inch above toe.

TASSEL
MAKE 2.

Cut 15 strands of dark orchid, each 7 inches long. Tie separate matching strand tightly around middle of all strands, fold strands in half. Tie another matching strand around all strands ¾ inch from top of fold, secure and hide ends inside Tassel. Trim all ends evenly.

Tie 1 Tassel to each end of Drawstring.

Fold Cuff down over Slipper. ■

Stitch Guide

For more complete information, visit **FreePatterns.com**

ABBREVIATIONS

beg	begin/begins/beginning
bpdc	back post double crochet
bpsc	back post single crochet
bptr	back post treble crochet
CC	contrasting color
ch(s)	chain(s)
ch-	refers to chain or space previously made (e.g., ch-1 space)
ch sp(s)	chain space(s)
cl(s)	cluster(s)
cm	centimeter(s)
dc	double crochet (singular/plural)
dc dec	double crochet 2 or more stitches together, as indicated
dec	decrease/decreases/decreasing
dtr	double treble crochet
ext	extended
fpdc	front post double crochet
fpsc	front post single crochet
fptr	front post treble crochet
g	gram(s)
hdc	half double crochet
hdc dec	half double crochet 2 or more stitches together, as indicated
inc	increase/increases/increasing
lp(s)	loop(s)
MC	main color
mm	millimeter(s)
oz	ounce(s)
pc	popcorn(s)
rem	remain/remains/remaining
rep(s)	repeat(s)
rnd(s)	round(s)
RS	right side
sc	single crochet (singular/plural)
sc dec	single crochet 2 or more stitches together, as indicated
sk	skip/skipped/skipping
sl st(s)	slip stitch(es)
sp(s)	space(s)/spaced
st(s)	stitch(es)
tog	together
tr	treble crochet
trtr	triple treble
WS	wrong side
yd(s)	yard(s)
yo	yarn over

Chain—ch: Yo, pull through lp on hook.

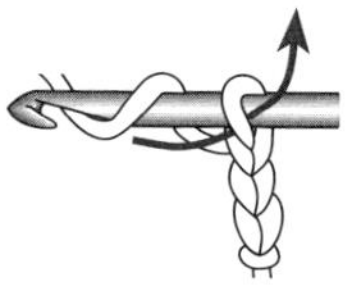

Slip stitch—sl st: Insert hook in st, pull through both lps on hook.

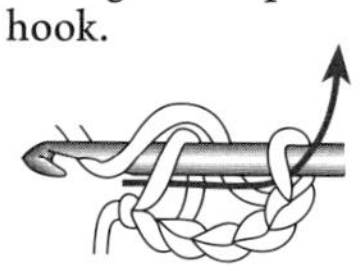

Single crochet—sc: Insert hook in st, yo, pull through st, yo, pull through both lps on hook.

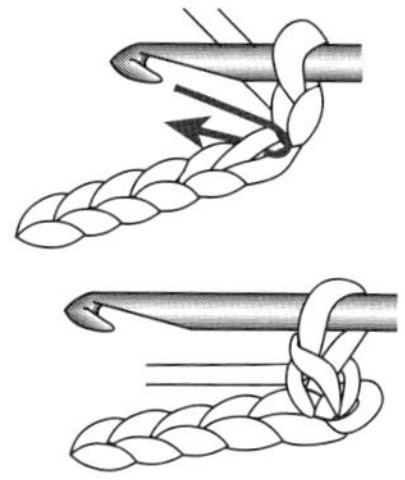

Front post stitch—fp:
Back post stitch—bp: When working post st, insert hook from right to left around post st on previous row.

Front loop—front lp
Back loop—back lp

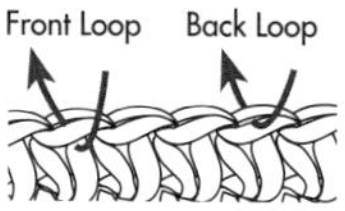

Half double crochet—hdc: Yo, insert hook in st, yo, pull through st, yo, pull through all 3 lps on hook.

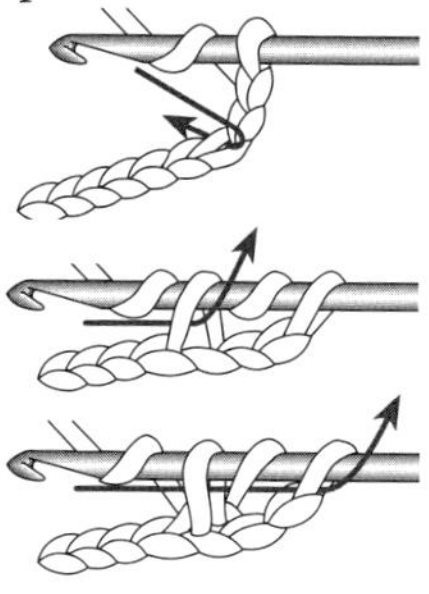

Double crochet—dc: Yo, insert hook in st, yo, pull through st, [yo, pull through 2 lps] twice.

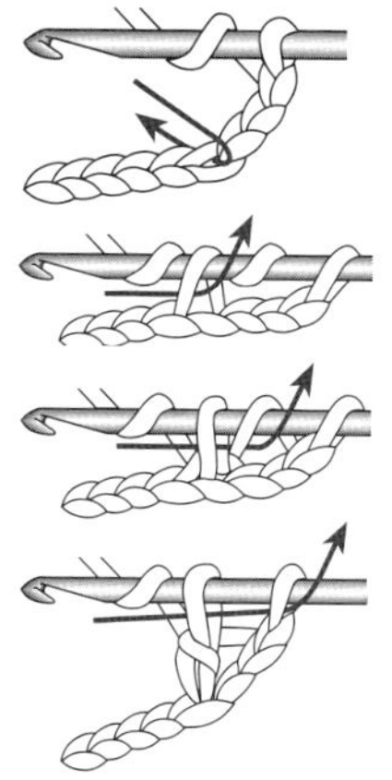

Change colors: Drop first color; with 2nd color, pull through last 2 lps of st.

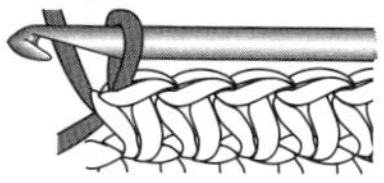

Treble crochet—tr: Yo twice, insert hook in st, yo, pull through st, [yo, pull through 2 lps] 3 times.

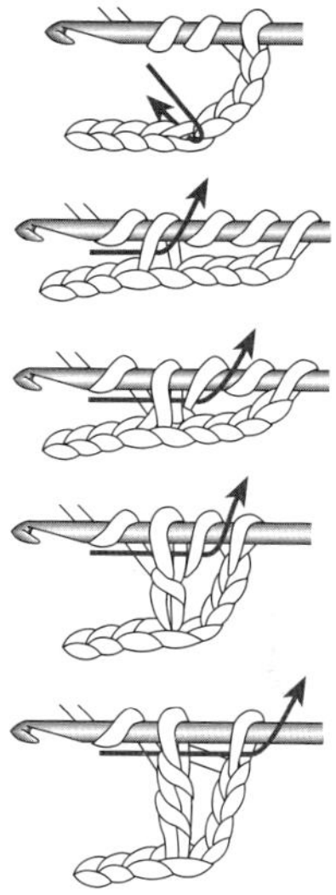

Double treble crochet—dtr: Yo 3 times, insert hook in st, yo, pull through st, [yo, pull through 2 lps] 4 times.

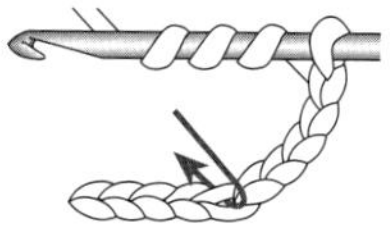

Single crochet decrease (sc dec): (Insert hook, yo, draw lp through) in each of the sts indicated, yo, draw through all lps on hook.

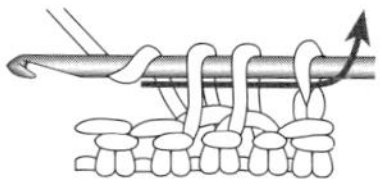

Example of 2-sc dec

Half double crochet decrease (hdc dec): (Yo, insert hook, yo, draw lp through) in each of the sts indicated, yo, draw through all lps on hook.

Example of 2-hdc dec

Double crochet decrease (dc dec): (Yo, insert hook, yo, draw loop through, draw through 2 lps on hook) in each of the sts indicated, yo, draw through all lps on hook.

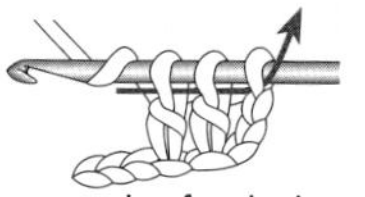

Example of 2-dc dec

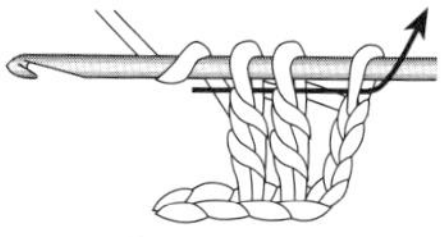

Example of 2-tr dec

Treble crochet decrease (tr dec): Holding back last lp of each st, tr in each of the sts indicated, yo, pull through all lps on hook.

US		UK
sl st (slip stitch)	=	sc (single crochet)
sc (single crochet)	=	dc (double crochet)
hdc (half double crochet)	=	htr (half treble crochet)
dc (double crochet)	=	tr (treble crochet)
tr (treble crochet)	=	dtr (double treble crochet)
dtr (double treble crochet)	=	ttr (triple treble crochet)
skip	=	miss

Annie's Attic®

TOLL-FREE ORDER LINE or to request a free catalog (800) LV-ANNIE (800) 582-6643
Customer Service (800) AT-ANNIE (800) 282-6643, **Fax** (800) 882-6643
Visit AnniesAttic.com

ISBN: 978-1-59635-232-2

Printed in USA

1 2 3 4 5 6 7 8 9